In Search of Stansylvania

FORTY-TWO POEMS

Stan Bell

SCHILTRON

In Search of Stansylvania: Forty-Two Poems

Published by
Schiltron
419 North Woodside Road
Kelvinbridge
Glasgow G20 6NN
0141 334 1485

ISBN 0-9552280-0-X

Typeset in Janson Text LT
Cover design and layout by Mary Patrick

SCHILTRON

For Cathie

Contents

THE EDGE *An Iomall*

Island Stories   1
Stornoway Easter   2
Ness Haiku / Haiku Nis   3
The Peats   4
Seabird   5
Island Treasures   6
Class War / Kelvin Event   7
On a Ness Beach   8
The Gift   9
Watching   10
The Embers Glow   11
The Stones of Callanish   12
Maps   13
Banners Bright   14

LIFE CLASS

With Mayakovsky In Mind   15
Life Class   16
Art World Signals   17
The Apples Of Paul Cezanne   18
The Dialectic   19
'D' for Decency   20
Landscape   21
Exhibition   22
Roman Records   23
The Alchemist   24
Monuments   25
Duck-Run   26
The Rainbow Bridge   27
Amber   28

December Dream	29
Ghost Dancing	30
Honey Pears	31
Quietly	32
No Mean Road	33
Belfast Bar	34
The Third Room	35
The Last Supper	36
Dream-Time In Dublin	37
Knotted String	38
Angel of the Toll	39
The Grove Stadium	40
Sunsets	41
The Proclamation	42

THE EDGE | *An Iomall*

Island Stories

Simple Geography should be sufficient
neither myth nor symbol
need embroider the wide sweep of ocean
nor sweeten the gannet's cry.

But still

There, an outline of yesterday's lazybeds
sketched-in by corn marigolds
and the hillock on the headland
hides a prehistoric pottery.

The beach appears now sea-washed smooth
but somewhere deep inscribed
a thousand keel ruts, keeping score
of surf-launched island boats.

The machair has its lovers' tales
every patch of moor is named
six close-grazed mounds, unmarked graves.
mementos of an Uigeach raid.

Simple geography should be sufficient
neither myth nor symbol
need enhance that rich inheritance.

But still

Every island stone
has at least
one island story.

Stornoway Easter

Even the agnostics
freely acknowledge
aspects of Easter.

New lambs on the croft
new grass on the grazings
the stale air of winter
redeemed by westerly winds.

Freely acknowledge
that the cold dark threat
has passed over
that open doors disclose
new etched horizons.

In Cromwell Street
a day-glo notice reads

GET YOUR EASTER BUNNY HERE

The rabbits lie flayed and livid
on the butcher's tray.

It is a joke of course
Stornwegians are like that.

Ness Haiku

Machair dress circle
Dell Rock centre of the blue stage
gannets dive on cue.

Haiku Nis

Na suidheachan as fhearr air a mhachair
Sgeir Dhail na theis-mheadhan an
    àrd-urlar ghorm
Na sùlairean a' caradh-fodha aig an dearbh
    àm cheart.

The Peats

The crofters slowly skim the land
two turfs measure cut each year
peat banks left like frozen waves
at intervals
across the moor.

Walls patterned by the rhythms
of the tairisgean's cutting edge
graphic witness
to hard won skill and sensibility.

Displaced turfs
redeem the open cut
countless minute shuttles
start the task
of weaving whole the land again.

Seabird

He lit
with clean grey
with bright white
the stained tone values
of the byre.

Alert but unafraid
with fisher's eye
made a cool appraisal
of the scouting cats.

A makeshift prison
with no horizon
with no sight
of star or shoreline.

Damaged wing
notwithstanding
no sheltering here
for a sea-sky raider.

No sheltering here
for an in-shore pirate.

Returned to the sea-edge
riding the swell
to the cry of the tern
his chances no worse than mine

when I tell her.

Island Treasures

They can be valuable
stones
if stones are
what you have.

Specials.

Lintels or hearthstones
marked on the moor
or river bed
sledged home.

How many re-builds ago?
How many fires?

The crofter reads
the Farmer's wall

(alive now with
chattering starlings)

Maggie-May's mother's
stones at the gate there.

Stones from Murdo's house
at the road.

A nice man the Farmer
right enough.

But Murdo's stones
are in his wall
Murdo's bones
are in his wall.

Class War

Symbol of power
an eagle glides in majesty
chased by common gulls.

Kelvin Event

The crane statuesque
a cormorant spreads his wings
and wins our applause.

On a Ness Beach

Pacing-out South Dell beach
each footprint cleanly etched
as a moon-man's mark.

The pulse and suck of the Atlantic
grinding shell, polishing pebbles
and milling sand.

Just within
wind-flickering earshot
urlar and variations
of an elusive pibroch.

West, beyond the water-colour smudge
of merging sea and sky
a new-found-land-fall.

A mere Faroes hop
Iceland skip
and Greenland jump away.

Another Hebron
a new, a seventh, city of refuge
for exiled Nisseachs.

The Gift
(for Basia)

You have a gift
with lucid words to clarify
the stammered fragments
of explanation.

With empathy
to resolve the ambiguities
the disordered elements
of the image.

To sense the rhythms
within the wild cacophony
of wind, wings and sea
lashed gannet rock.

See the harmony
in the old confused rituals
the raw scrabbling courage
of the guga hunt.

You have the gift
of song.

Watching

Watching you watching

Silvered gulls
settle on the hillside
above Dell River

They
dream of breaking fast
with morning trout

You
edged by June night-light
embrace the moment.

The Embers Glow

Time was like good peats
we burned bright with flames
enough to light the corries

Now glowing red
warming the long evening

A new morning will find
the embers smouldering still
with persistent promise.

The Stones Of Callanish

Before the stones
this land was sacred
a melding of the elements
air, earth and water, gilded
by the pale fire of the sun.

Before the stones
the land was sacred
centre-point for the circling
eagles asserting dominion
over their fiefdom.

Before the stones
the land was sacred
an altar for the First-Ones
offering their best-loved, ensuring
re-emergence of the light.

Before the stones
the land was sacred
threshold for the Shaman's
journeys to the nether-world
of the five kingdoms.

The Wise-Ones knew
this land was sacred
ordained site of the stones
their cosmological machine
to measure time; to track the heavens.

Bridgehead to the infinite
this land is sacred
Stones, Altar, Shaman and Eagle
conduits of the spirit, linking
the earthbound to the eternal.

Maps
(for Sally)

We each make our own map
although the starting point
is sometimes given.

My own compass points
are some second-hand bookshops where
sales are the only seasons.

(Who was it that said
wherever you go in the world
you must pass through Barvas?)

A Birthday, like Barvas
grid reference on a time-map
is a gate-way to many journeys.

With your special gifts
affinity with celestial navigation
a sureness of touch.

You are certain to visit
many shining cities.

Banner Bright

Time, love and sharing
have made of us
the warp and weft of
a seamless fabric
made of us the one whole cloth.

Woven tight as any good tweed
stretched between the poles
of a long life
made of us a banner bright.

With memory-symbols
and treasured icons
resplendent as the sun banners
of the Fianna
made of us a woven poem.

Made of us a banner bright.

Life Class

With Mayakovsky in Mind

Even as we first made use
of plumb-bob and chalk-line
mundane tools of mural making
we had Mayakovsky in mind.

We adopted as our own
his manifesto
"the streets are our paint brushes
the squares are our palettes".

The implacable artist
the barricade poet
rode the white water of revolution
deployed word and image
against the White Guards.

Our foes mere city planners
our aims more modest
to enhance the environment to give
Glasgow bright singing walls.

We shared his belief in the
magic of colour
the power of design
redemption of all things by art.

In getting out of the gallery
And into the street
We had Mayakovsky in mind.

Life Class

The model is late
sleep smudged, defenceless droop
deflecting all rebuke.

The pose is set
fixed by chalk on throne and dais
easels scrape in place.

First sight-lines plotted
points of reference set down
with tentative marks.

Eye and hand together
discern shapes, establish values
discount thrown shadows.

Seeking to reconcile
the given laws of light, of form
with living movement.

With a sniper's intensity
striving to see through and into
that... that which is unique.

Art World Signals

The artist claimed
that 'all art aspires
to the condition of music'
to complete autonomy.

That despite the seaport setting
his mural was abstract
all references were internal
contained no maritime image
carried no message.

A sea-going man
admiring the painting
claimed that in the colour composition
he found many nautical shapes

In the top left quarter
a blue and yellow signal flag
when flown at sea
has an unambiguous meaning
it reads:

I WISH TO COMMUNICATE WITH YOU.

The Apples of Paul Cezanne

It started in Aix
it started with apples
cone, cylinder, sphere
geometry of form.

With tone, with colour
epiphanous structures
new art for an era
visual perceptions re-focussed.

Vasarely's monument
to art's constant elements
stands in the shadow
of Mont Saint-Victoire.

Creation's equations
past, present and future
found resolution

in the apples of
Paul Cezanne.

The Dialectic
(for Bracaval)

Within the paintings
the dialectic operates.

Dynamics of light
set against darkness
movement opposed to stasis.

A contrast of tones and textures
of the rational and free expression.

Hexagonal forms
product of external pressures
constraint random chaos.

Within the paintings
synthesis and harmony are found.

Geometry sustains
Camille Pissarro's dream.

Sympathetic structures
balance of Order and Liberty
make possible the Anarchist Ideal.

D for Decency

(on the painting by Bill Gallacher)

His courage was never in doubt
nor his honesty questioned
he made a choice
between history and love.

He chose love

Later his grandchildren asked
about the D-shaped scar
livid against the pale of his back
that is a D for Decency.

He would laugh

Long afterwards they learned
hot iron had seared his skin
his regiment had branded him
the juggernaut of history
had been offended.

Landscape
for James Robertson

Each painting an open door
to an unknown universe
landscape... yet emphatically

not scenery.

An invitation to witness
this artist's vision
landscape in form, in content

painted meditation.

Colour shape and texture
marks in rich profusion
confer upon us Right of Entry.

To this, his, other world.

Exhibition
(for Neil)

The setting
Heart-space of The Mackintosh
harled stone, stained timber
product of Scottish utility
Japanese fantasy
sacred talent.

The work:
Painted evocation of the sea-edge
surge-drag of Gaia's pulse
shifting shapes emerging
colours, fathoms blue
to sandbar green.
reflected light refracted
whispering shingle music
sea dreaming sea.

Even the maimed Victory
raises a wing in salutation
as do I.

Roman Records

On the Appian Way
near the Baths of Caracalla
mosaic panels record
the growth of Roman power

White tesserae on black

The first shows Rome
a pale dot
then stage by inexorable stage
light overwhelms the dark

On the final panel
the known world is Roman white

With some exceptions

On the North Western edge
beyond the rim of empire
a gold/black Caledonia
remains unbleached

I liked that, it seemed good
to be in the black.

The Alchemist
(In memory of Colin)

As a hillside burn in spate
draws on every source
lochan, spring, rockpool and overspill
feeding the brown torrent
brawling through heather-roots and bracken
to emerge, at last, silver treasure.

So this magus turned artist
conjured up sources
from art and nature's vast portfolios
shoreline textures, poetry and driftwood
fact, fantasy and moorland bird-bone.

Methods equally diverse
woodblock, letterform
brushed pigment and wing-tipped line
craftsman's cunning and blackart alchemy
he created a precious stream.

Of timeless visual poetry.

Monuments

The iconoclasts are busy

heroes plucked wholesale

from their pedestals

mosaic images chipped

from Metro station walls

a frenzy of renaming

squares, streets, towns

and cities

plinths remain empty

idle sculptors wait in vain

for inspiration.

Duck-Run and Puppet Theatre
(Four sketches and a CODA)

With every saw-cut it became clearer
it was a dream trap we were making
the ducks were a lure
the chicken-wire a snare to braid
the gold of your compassion.

Your vision and my sawing
created this ramshackle crate
your persistence and my compliance
could lift it
and fly us to the Butt.

I admire your way
with oval sprigs, stroking them in
with a joiner's competence
gilding every task
with bright eyed optimism.

In the coloured booth
with a playboard for your dreams
I'd be a glove on your supple hand
I suspect that I would end dangling
from that gibbet of my own devising.

CODA

It is evidently true that I make boxes
for the girls I love, or lock them
in back rooms 'inadvertently'
that given enough two by twos
I would make a doo`cot
of the world.

The Rainbow Bridge
(for a birthday)

It's a nice age to reach
a bridge to be crossed
a rainbow bridge.

Still time for rehearsals of course
the script far from complete
but already the poet
reaches for his pen
the mandolin comes off the wall
fresh colour squeezed on the palette.

Your crossing will be marked
by brighter stars
and new minted dreams.

Amber

For Cathie

It did seem a suitable present
to bring from Leningrad
(as it then was)
an amber bracelet.

I had thought of you as I walked
by the frozen edge of the Finland gulf
and as I scuffed the sky-washed snow
in the pine forest
around Ilya Repin's dacha.

You always were the golden girl of course
but there in the crystal cold
in the resin-scented frost
pale amber seemed more accurate.

Warmer and softer than the metal
every bit as durable
product of sunshine and growth
enriched with countless fragments
of a shared life.

Gallimaufry

December Dream

At what had been the Moscow home
of a Decembrist conspirator
the arcane complexities of the Academy
are carefully collated
in Kropotkinskaya Street.

Negotiations are now complete
the documents to be signed
our colleagues arrange a special treat
for us, their Scottish guests.

Preserved intact within the house
the Decembrists' hidden room
we hold our ceremony here where Democrats
conspired against the Czar.

The young man from the Ministry
in spite of our clowning at the secret door
remains dignified and solemn as befits
this place that led to martyrdom.

It is Nineteen-Eighty-Nine
the October-Dream is all but dead, withered
by the scourging winds of sacrifice.

But somehow...
the December-Dream persists

in Kropotkinskaya Street.

Ghost Dancing

Are we Ghost-Dancing?

Praying that the next sunrise
will glint on the banners
of the Fianna.

Are we Ghost-Dancing?

Hoping that our chanted slogans
will re-animate the dour ranks
of the Schiltrons.

Are we Ghost-Dancing?

Dreaming that our ritual stamping
will recreate the miracle
of Athelstaneford.

Doubting our own substance

Are we Ghost-Dancing?

Honey Pears

We feel the need to strike a blow
to raise a cry, which out-performs
our newly broken voices.

Our slogan SUAS ALBA with lion rampant
we will blaze along the parapet
of a city centre bridge.

Traitors will falter patriots cheer
well maybe, their eyes for the road
empowerment is ours alone.

Aspiring artists sketch a measured plan
choose appropriate letter-forms
cut a lion-shape stencil.

Come night we work with quiet intensity
ruler, chalk, paint and brush
clean lines and sweeping serifs.

Lookouts deployed at four corners
our agreed warning signal
a street vendor's cry 'Honey Pers'

There it is now 'HONEY PERS'! 'HONEY PERS'!
tools packed well rehearsed scramble
we're off - - - clear away 'HONEY PERS'!

But - - - our vanity betrays us, our need
to dot our I's and sweeten our lines
ensures our certain capture.

Even so the fine was surely worth it
the message there ten years or more.

SUAS ALBA!
SUAS ALBA!

Quietly

In the tenement quiet
we are startled awake.

The sound
an unmistakable mix
of rattle, scrape
and pulley-wheel squeak.

A window-sash
lifted with tentative care
not ours, but near, quite near.

The silence
suspended by a fluttering rush
then a heavy but soft padded thud.

An old carpet dumped
the silence restored
we are now reassured.

But no - - - we knew
(as we all know who listen).

A neighbour
who had always lived quietly
had now quietly flown.

In the tenement dark.

No Mean Road

From Lansdowne Kirk at Kelvinbridge
with its tallest slimmest spire
needling the underside of heaven
it's no mean road.

The wax-fruit terrace McCrone depicts
first step up or last step down
for Glasgow's middle-class contenders
it's no mean road.

Here William Smith first formed-fours
his Boys' Brigade paraded
bugles playing 'Sure and Stedfast'
it's no mean road.

The Pewter Pot where painters met
while a knowledge of Kenneths expounded
MacDiarmid swapped stanzas with Scott
it's no mean road.

Fragments remain of Lyon Street
Hero Street of World War One
a short street with a gey long death list
it's no mean road.

Saint Joseph's at the Canal dead-end
Gerard Manley Hopkins once held Mass
tending his inscape of shining words
it's no mean road.

'Horseback brown' Kelvin tunnels through trees
salmon have started to spawn again
the Kelvin Walkway leads to the hills
it is no mean road.

North Woodside Road.

Belfast Bar 1976

All agreed
it was neutral ground
used by both sides.

She is apolitical
he is a tourist.

Fuelled by vodka and vanity
he makes his point
with unintended vehemence.

"THE PROTESTANTS HAVE
HAD THEIR CHANCE!"

In the sudden glassy silence
she makes her point
with quiet insistence.

"Look out for the four boys
in the corner
drinking orange juice".

The Third Room

They are to be found
in the third room of memory
at best, ambiguous heroes.

Soldiers of the shadows
artisans of urban conflict
who killed and maimed for The Cause.

Icons of The Liberation
to be found a place in the Red Corner
or dismissed
as clowns in death-masks.

They wait half-forgotten
in History's long spiralling loop
for the victor's partial judgement.

The Last Supper

We read each book hoping
as we thumb the pages
that somehow the author too
is within our grasp.

And value artwork most
on which the artist's hand
has left its mark
the better to possess him.

The Makar must have known
as he handed round
the bread and wine
that these alone could never
assuage our hunger.

Dream-Time in Dublin

Closing time in dream-time Dublin
outside on O'Donohue's winter pavement
Ted Fury plays 'Hares on the Mountain'
backed by the spoons and clapping.

Amid the craic a folk-club's named
fiddling and jigging Ted leads off
in dream-time we follow with the others
dancing through the frosted grass
along the edge of St. Stephen's green.

With glowing cigarette ends
we draw ploughs against the sky
always finding matching stars.

In dream-time we compete in the choruses
failing to out-sing the singers.

And later

Sharing in the emotional charge
we stand and sing the 'Soldiers Song'.

And later still
I kiss wet snowflakes
from your face.

In dream-time Dublin.

Knotted String

If all recorded memories were kept
as lengths of knotted string
ours would be
gey long.

We could search the line to find
that scrabble of knots, telling
of our canoe trip down Loch Sheil
to the sea.

Describing that magic moment
when the rainbow, a 'bow in the cloud'
seemed to arc from our tent pole
to Acharacle.

Of Clanranald's burial isle, bracken
free but crowded with dream bait
Finnan's stone alter with the pilgrim's
unrung bell.

And at the mouth of Sheil River
being lifted by the slow sea-swell
canoe skin flexing against thigh
free of the sandbar to merge at last
with the sea-wet sky.

Between the knots there would be
only the smooth sweet texture of
closely twisted strands. Even so
these .... these would represent
the best times.

Angel of the Toll

A quarter of a mile apart
we played many of the same games
we kicked the can and chased our girds
roller-skated on the smooth asphalt.

Took our chances on the leaps
dreeps and jumps, as closely graded
as a climber's rock-face route
claimed our streets singing 'We Won the War'.

Looking down to the river
we shared the sight of our guardian angel
pointed wings scraping smoke stained clouds
the Angel of the Toll staring fiercely East.

On guard against Gorbals marauders
surviving German bombs and wrecker's hammer
there still, bright with fresh re-gilding
just one of the jewels in our plaited memories.

The Grove Stadium

Only in Glasgow
could a Presbyterian Kirk
be so smoothly converted
to a boxing arena.

And regular venue
for Anarchist sermons
preached with passion
laced with humour.

A radical change
pulpit, lectern abandoned
front pews realigned
the square ring constructed.

Dour conventicle
where prophets were invoked
saintly fighters now use ringcraft
to avoid martyrdom.

Anarchist angels floodlit
and ring-rope framed
summon the spirits of Godwin
Tolstoy and Kropotkin.

Only in Glasgow do Anarchists
preach peace on stained canvas
behind ropes; The Way Utopian
                The Word Liberty.

The boxers refuse to be drawn
four hard rounds being more
than enough to be going on with.

Sunsets

We share sunsets
drawing each other's attention
to nuances of colour
light enhanced cloud-forms.

A sense of urgency
informs our appreciation
conscious of impermanence
of transient beauty.

No need for words
impossible to articulate
(except by the wine-buffs lexicon)
such shot-silk subtlety.

We share a sunset
making for our own horizon
enjoying the slow spin to the light
with still no need for words.

The Proclamation

No time:

To wait, debate, to consolidate
resolve conflicting interests
take into account innumerable shades
and tints of opinion.

No time to contrive
a consensual compromise.

Time now:

To create, make, to fabricate
setting aside strategic arguments
reach for the unpublished manuscript
reject the Canon.

Time:

To declare, announce, to inaugurate
independence, self-governing status
proclaim, the sovereign, the autonomous
Republic of Stansylvania.

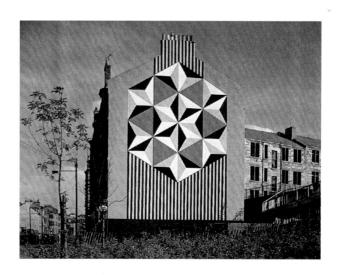

About Stan Bell

As well as writing poetry Stan Bell is also a visual artist and has therefore a natural interest in the connections between text and image. He is a Glaswegian but with family connections in the Isle of Lewis where he has been a frequent visitor and has become increasingly interested in the organic aesthetic of the Western Isles. His poetry has appeared in a number of publications including *Coincidence*; *Circles and Lines*; *Skinklin Star* and *La Fabrique*.

The cover image and all images within the book are of artworks by Stan Bell.

The Gaelic version of *Ness Haiku* was composed by Evelyn Coull.